This Arc of Assurances

This Arc of Assurances
poems

Martha Fox

GRAYSON BOOKS
West Hartford, Connecticut
graysonbooks.com

For Gregg
Again and always

Acknowledgments

Gratitude to Rod Kessler for deft editing and heartening conversation.
And to Cape Ann Poets for prompts and responses reflected in these poems.

Sincere thanks to the following authors for inspiring language and form:

"Love Poem" was nudged by Ronald Brownstein's *Rock Me on the Water*.
"When I chose you, I did not know" takes a line from songwriter Alain Cavé.
"Lament" borrows images from Valeria Luiselli's stunning novel *Lost Children Archive*.
"Comme il pleut sur la ville" refers to a poem by Paul Verlaine.
"Once" remembers the essay "I Remember Nothing" by Nora Ephron.
"In it Together" spins off "Everything is Waiting for You" by David Whyte.
The prologue of "Hometown" contains details from Marshall Swan's history *Town on Sandy Bay*.
"The Current Satan" is an affectionate nod to my late friend Thomas Lux.

"You rise before the roosters to take on dangerous roads" is a cento, created from lines by these global poets:
Melissa Beauvery, Haiti "Famn Kanson"
Tuvia Ruebner, Israel "When I Arrived the Place Was;" "Farewell, Thank You."
Patricia Jabbeh Wesley, Liberia "Liberia;" "I Now Wander"
Yehuda Amichai, Israel "God-full-of-Mercy"
Mahmoud Darwish, Palestine "I Am From There;" "In Egypt"
Zeki Madjid, Syria "Dancing in the Olive Field"
Asmir Kujovic, Bosnia "That Day"
Haki Madhubuti, Rwanda "Rwanda: Where Tears Have No Power"
Elisha Porat, Israel "Khamsin on the Hills"
Suji Kwok Kim, Korea "Rice Field Road at Dusk;" "Montage with Neon, Bok Choi, Gasoline, Lovers & Strangers"
Goran Simic, Bosnia "The Sorrow of Sarajevo"
Najat Samad, Syria "When I am Overcome by Weakness"
Vonani Bila, South Africa "Give Me Love Rwanda"
Ketty Nivyabandi, Burundi "Les Petites Hommes"
Redempta Asifiwe, Rwanda "Silence"
Andreas Morgner, U.S.A "Ituri Province, D.R. Congo"

Grateful acknowledgment is made to the following publications in which these poems appeared:

Tide Lines: An Anthology of Cape Ann Poets: "Biography of a Wave, "A Man Who Digs Clams In Winter," "Steel Derrick Quarry, Autumn," "Whales in the Quarry," "Never in One Place at One Time," "Winter's End," and "Pueblos Blancos of Andalucía"
Comstock Review: "Empty"
Voices and Verse: "Quarry Walk"
Writer's Digest: "Lament" Third Prize Winner Best Poem 2021

Contents

Never In One Place at One Time

Love Poem

Waiting for you to wake,
I'm sipping west coast coffee, reading about LA
in '74. It was a pop Paris-in-the-20s:
Archie Bunker, "China Town," and Jackson Browne.
Our anthem—"Rock Me on the Water."
Honey, you rocked me on the water
bed every night, and every day
we hung on the fringe of The Biz.
I drove my grandma's Ford bequest to the studio,
sliding into a slot with my name on it, comped
by my boss, a mean (albeit famous) comedian.
I'd stride through the lot in my one pair of fancy pants—
thrift-shop Missonis. Gaffers and gofers looked.
I left them behind with a whiff of Rive Gauche.
In the office, my anything-for-a-laugh employer,
would trill to his sycophants (lesser but equally mean
comedians), "Ooo, la la. Eau de French whore!"
I'd laugh along with them, as I was underpaid to do.
At night, I yanked the darts from my feckless heart
while we slugged jug Almaden in front of the TV,
bingeing Patty Hearst. I was transfixed
by my almost-age-mate, both of us girls
feigning grown-up, living in sin with bespectacled
preppies, both lost as the linear narrative
of our families' expectations. Kidnapped.
A blur of years before, my own captor a manic
just back from 'Nam but not back from trauma.
Needing a girl to save him, he grabbed me
on my way to the early shift. Raving about
Zippo raids, he drove me around Cambridge
for an eon of hours, a knife on his thigh, until I
promised to meet him for dinner. "I love you,
but I need to change my dress," I reasoned.

13

He dropped me off at home. Later, I wailed,
"I lied!" when cops popped out
of an azalea cloud to cuff him. I did as Patty
said, "accommodate my thoughts" to his.
After 58 days of rape, harangue and closet,
Patty grabbed a semi-automatic and a nom de guerre,
and shot a storefront up. She covered the comrades.
The jury scoffed, could not believe
what put guns in her hand, slogans in her throat
was terror. Only when the verdict came down,
did I tell my own "catch and release" drama to you.
Your eyes filled. You called me brave
for saving my own life. You said the same thing
40 years later, when I drifted back
from anesthesia, having whispered to the surgeon
fixing to carve a notch in my breast, "Take everything.
I only want to live."
Oh, what people do to save their lives! We conspire,
con, and crush. Tell and fall for big lies.
Some for the kingdom and the power and the glory,
but most, just for the breathing.
I thought of Patty once since her pardon,
when her bulldogs won double at Westminster.
Sitting here this morning, I consider what I won.
Decades of one-more days. And what I've done
for each of those. For the sun and the sparrows
and waiting for you to wake and kiss me.
I will stop at nothing.

To My Teenage Boy

How you loved summer night storms!
Black gusts swiping at treetops,
clouds like frantic rags scrubbing
the stained moon.

The younger one cried
for us, but you rose
from your bed, in thrall to
the howl of air against house,
pressing your face to the glass,
flushing with the pressure of
wind from the Caribbean.

And those savage nor'easters in winter?
You'd laugh at the granite's shudder
along the Atlantic path.
While breakers tossed boulders
like your magic pebbles,
you'd shove your face into
the drenching gale,
struggling against my grasp
to reach out for
the treacherous sea.

In the tempest of your adolescence,
you refuge in a room of wall-to-wall
contradictions: soccer balls, poetry books,
posters romanticizing fame and pain.
You bury your face in the pillow
that might as well be a white-out
blizzard in which you could walk
away from the well-lit house
toward the broken seawall

where the bay bleeds and
recedes and you
disappear
just like that…

Why I Love Dreams

"When I waked, I cried to dream again."
—Shakespeare, *The Tempest*

Our lost ones may sometimes appear. Last night,
you walked with me on Craggy Gardens trail
where rhododendrons' guileless faces shone,
twangling like the dandelion tucked behind your ear.

Unhidden then, my tears filled your cupped palms
as clear as Nantahala's pools, and when
those might-have-beens had run the rapids of
your opened hands, I heard you laugh!

The night before, I did not sleep. I remembered
the bellow of a cow crying *Come back*
to her calf over the yowl of the coyote pack.
Her milk moaning in her udder, splashing on the grass.

Let me sleep —
        The enormity of *Never* never ends.
Oh, let me dream—
                The only way I might see you again.

Note: The Nantahala is a white-water river in western North Carolina.

In the Cathedral of St. John the Divine

Quartz Crystal Cluster
2000 Pounds, 200 Million Years Old

Jagged mutant cocoon,
the crystal languishes in a giant case
of exhausted air.

I recall a hundred-year-old lobster
in a tank like this, one baseball-mitt claw
outstretched toward us gawkers.

100 years in the lap and hug of
rockweed, in the sway of historic hurricanes.
To have swum so long in phosphorescence,
passing up the trappers' bait!

This crystal, caged in an urban corner,
is lighted electrically, its prism points like
skyscrapers uprooted by modernist sculptors.

The quartz is as pallid as a corpse
in a fluorescent morgue.
Embedded splashes and streaks of rust
evidence of some past hemorrhage.

More bizarre, on the cage's floor
shine pennies shoved through uncaulked cracks
as if this chip of planet were some wishing well
granting whims for love and money.

I say, if this wretched relic could do that,
it would wish itself back in the Arkansas ledge
where it was captured like an unlucky lobster.

It would settle itself under eons of rain-cool
sediment, nestle in with a Pompeii of slugs and fossils.
It would sigh the way a stone sighs when it sinks
into the quarry where it was born.

This hunk of rock would go home,
climb into its familiar lumpy bed,
sleep the sleep it was given,
and dream of its mother's youth.

Still Life with Bathtub Madonna

At the place in the dream
where someone I ache for appears
to lock eyes with me, I wake.

I turn to you. Your tangled landscape –
blanket, shoulder, back – is abstract
and apparently still? Breathless,

I see you through one eye, through
the wrong end of a telescope.
I squint for visible rib-rise.

Of course, warm to the touch, you are
alive, and so am I, but how
precariously!

I rise to lean against the sill.
Out our frosted window
gaudy stars stare back.

Below, in the neighbor's yard,
Mary flares in her electric cerulean arch.
Everything regards everything else.

Never in One Place at One Time

Clusters of lavender asters bend
frayed, fringed heads into Pasture Road.
Afternoon: every window closes darkness in.
Moving out of shadow twigs, I'm sunlit.
Think of singing, but don't quite dare.

I feel I'm eight again and school's out.
Leaves give off the copper smell of tea
steeping in my grandmother's cup,
that brown of mahogany desk where I sound
out, on her letterhead, notes to my dead father.

Into shush of chestnut dust and footfall,
waves erode rock, design beaches.
Beyond the bay, a horizon torn from sky.
How glad I am—to live in a thin place,
a place unconstrained and full of time.

How opened my daughter will feel,
bending to a last October rose whose petals hold
the scent of her great-grandmother's cheek,
walking to a town where, when she looks out,
the breakwater marks her place in the world.

On some beneficent autumn afternoon,
my child will say as I do now,
My mother would have loved this day.

Museum of Childhood: Closed

Sign seen near West Ossippee, New Hampshire

A stone shed.
Mullioned windows opaque
with cobwebs and mold.

What varieties of snow days,
bruises, disses, and spitty secrets
are curated here?

I imagine fragile invaluables
cram smudged display cases labeled: "Carefree,"
"Not Fair," and "Pinkie Swear."

Maybe a craggy caretaker will pause a push mower
to say the curator hasn't shown up for weeks,
talk a bit of trash about him…

Lanky guy with comic book eyes
and wisps of Disney color in his hair.
Sleeps in, doesn't give a crap

yet about the relics of his own life,
even as he hoards them,
even as they endure his disdain.

Winter's End

*"The soil is the great connector of lives,
the source and destination of all."* —*Wendell Berry*

1.
The yard is haggard
and my house a weathered face.
Faded, the clustered village:
a smudge of wood smoke
and exhaust from the snow's slow melt.

Winter's burned out by wind
from the west, the stuffy breath
of cities we islanders disdain—
congestion and combustion.
The last flakes of the season
fall to earth like ash.

2.
Four centuries ago, first settlers' oxen,
flanks dripping, worked this month's mud
in chains, yanking boulders like molars
from their sockets, leveraging stones
to define our yards.

Through sepia years, their heirs planted
orchards, fine brush strokes in the pasture
on the drumlin above the cove.

3.
Our grown children rake last fall's leaves,
storm-swept against the stone wall, helping us
old folks, shushing our protest. I follow them past

my reflection on the window. Return to dust?
Even my babies?

One day, the equinox balances
dusk and dawn. Nature's repentant
rotation wakes snowdrop and daffodil
from frosted root and fiber. This soil—
solid, liquid, gas—grounds them
as they blossom, swaddles them
while they rest, absorbs them
when they're finished, as it did
the first flaring, fertile stars.

The Second Stage of Grief

Her dark-circled eyes
dart like panic
in the loud gusts of jargon.

She hears only the surgeon's
"Tough day!" as, later, he
pours vodka for his lover.

She is the "Patient's Spouse."
Her head whirls way around
at laughter in the corridor.

Now, her arms unfold a cape
of wings to cover her
husband who shudders

in the stillness that is
the eye of the goddamned
white-coat's words.

Empty

as the highway at 2 a.m.
and the blank moon it chases
as the talk radio demigod
and the long night of his listeners
as the boney arms of the December tree
in the dark yard of my own dark
home.

Not the emptiness of a wine bottle
overturned in a silver bucket,
of a windy beach combed
by night's high tide. No, not
the emptiness after tangled sighs
in saxophone evenings.

Not even the emptiness of this
white paper, pale as the exhausted stars,
as my mirror face, as the hospital
corridor of doors. But more—
empty as I am
to see your eyes so full
of fear.

Trying on a New Behavior

Light-hearted for once, I decide to overcome death.
Why draft my last gasped words at dawn;
my recent physical was passable. Why
revise that eulogy while pumping gas?
Lay a kayak paddle on a jumble of Teddy Bears
at my son's imagined makeshift memorial?

I choose to abandon my practice of practicing
grief. I will not stiffen my spine at the mirror,
prepping for celebrations of life, nor will I
jot down "Possible Impending Dooms."
Our social circle seems okay today.

I drive home after a draft beer or three
with a long-lost friend. The moon's a specter
behind eerie clouds. I don't pretend it's full
of meaning—just tap the steering wheel
to Country Classics.

Tonight, no method-acting tears in the
driveway of our incandescent house.
I plan: tomorrow I'll wake refreshed
and continue to make nothing
of nothingness.

The Management of Pain

1.

Aren't you numb enough yet? They spike morphine,
oxy, dilaudid, tramadol. They lay on heat and ice.
They shove everything they've got up against
your more-than-10-sized pain—syringe to blood to brain.
On the fog-colored wall, on the flat-screen TV,
a hollow man claims, "This is going to disappear."
Our age-mate in bed B yells, "Four more years!"
I can't translate the babble behind your eyes.
If God is doing his best in a broken world,
why are you so broken?

2.

With the cubicle curtain drawn, it's day and night and neither.
A slash of light across tan ceiling tiles is dawn and street lamp.
Everything's closed except your mouth, which is dry.
Remember the black-tail rabbit in Joshua Tree?
How he stared at us, all *Alice in Wonderland*—
"Oh, dear, oh dear, I shall be late."
Nowhere to hurry off to now.
Remember the kiln of that place? It glazed our eyes.
How stoned were we? It was the 70s,
and we were in our 20s, taking a break from jeering
"Peace & Love" at the troops just back from 'Nam.
Now we toss with shame, with tinnitus
of our unkindness at 2 a.m.

3.

The righteousness wore off. Commutes to the office and carpools
to the kids' schools, teacher conferences, and friends' transplants.
A bone-achy rage in us—the country we did not know well
enough to save enough is all but choking. We look on.

We cope. We garden, mow, mask up, and go to church.
We draft our obituaries, omitting disappointments.

4.
Your fractures hum like synthesizers. Your heart is a drum machine.
I watch it work the screen above your head. Your color is better.
But there are occlusion alarms, carts of cooked carrots
and computers clacking down the hall, a chuckle
from the nurses' station. What could possibly be funny?
There's a smear of blood on the linoleum.
My soles squeak out the door.

5.
At home, too many miles from the hospital, an orange moon rolls
like an August peach from the horizon. What should I do with this
harvest, all by myself? My words on a page are a poor substitute for you.
We've built a house. We've waltzed in the kitchen. We've believed
we'd manage even if the better angels crash and burn.
On the jagged path from passion for each other
to lust for time together, we've stumbled our way along.
Two on the head of a pin.

In The Cove

Old ghosts imprinted a watermark on this village.
We write their stories over it,
filling in blanks, inventing motives.

We revise with indelible ink; their sins
invent our motives. In kitchens
and front parlors, ghosts' heirs tangle

with genetics—dominant eyes and recessive
neuroses—*so* tangled. My neighbor stirs something
at a stove. Her girl's face flickers TV blue.

Slipped over the sill, the scent of stew simmering
stirs me, and blues—a remix of a woman crying out
her hunger to an empty room.

Some newcomers coddle familiars to warm
their empty rooms. Sometimes this muddle confuses,
swirling above rooftops in chimney smoke.

Once, under the rafters, in a muddle of unsettled bills
and dust-mote smoke, a boy wrote in his notebook.
He wrote, "My father left in a car."

Later, the boy, turned father, locked the garage door,
wrote a note, started his car.

Comme il pleut sur la ville

As it rains on the town,
I remember reciting my first French poem.
Verlaine, 8th grade, and Madame Echardt
     (*Répétez "langueur"* three times)

Such urgency then to feel

     lust's lucid music, full down-there
     theatrics in a fogged-up car
     thrusting toward some shimmering brink
       (So few things become what we imagine)

       to feel

     even agony's adrenaline
     the rasp of rumor, the lover leaving
     you disappearing like a smoldering cigarette
       (Always awaiting the worst pain)

Rain, falling, filled the poet's decadent heart

Decades later, I'm sitting still
at an open window, relieved
of ardor and anguish, overlooking
     my hill, wallowing in solitude

Rain falling, fills the morning's corridor

veils the neighbors' porches
polishes the quiet street
patters on the absinthe pond
       (Oh, Prince of Poets, time is the one
         reliable narcotic!)

Rain, filling the darkness falling

weights my hands
slows my pulse
bows my head

> *Langueur. Langueur. Langueur.*

The Things I Cannot Change

Hot Spell

For a week, we wake sticky to languid dawns,
pallid shadows, and incantations of ashen crows
cawing at the cauldron of the yard.

Afternoons, we wallow, all eyes and nostrils
above the quarry water's fevered skin.
Keloid earthworms scar granite ledges.
Bullfrogs fat on algae and skinny minnows
simmer in the shallows at the feet of
the stricken—I swear I see

George tiptoeing behind his kneeling Lennie
a woman wringing out rags in a hippo's path
the retired teacher reaching to strangle
the whiney boy in the blue swimsuit
or his heedless mother.

Evenings, katydids and crickets chant under the news:
magical thinkers turning their pockets inside out—
no more abracadabras there.
The bones of scientists glow in the black chasm
of distrust where they were tossed by oh-so-many of us.

Yes, tomorrow might send a shady cloud and a cooler wind.
Wisdom, who constructed the god that burrows
beneath our ribcage, might invent words to charm
us to change. But—

for the rest of the summer, I will imagine the end
of Earth, our incalescent planet, blue as flame's core.

I'll picture us standing hand in hand on the glassy sand,
hearing our desiccating hearts, staring

out past memorials to ice caps,
out where the horizon levitates
as heat waves build and wait,
out way farther than the eyes of the moon can see.

Biography of a Wave

The wave got her start
with a shove in the dark.
West of Lisbon, she was
a single silver glint
off Costa da Caparica,
slick with jet exhaust,
flecked with midnight's
cigarettes and condoms.

When asked, the wave tossed
off her edgy adolescence
moon-high in a tousled fetch.
She refused comment
on an infant swept away,
then vamped mid-Atlantic
cresting voluptuously,
commanding sailors' attention.

Toward the end, the old dame
was blowzy in diamonds
from the *Crystal Cloud*'s deck,
maudlin as boozy camaraderie,
a wrinkled sheet on the sea.
She lived, and then she broke
into a frothy song drowned
out by her smooth-faced sisters.

Cold War Bomb Shelter

Quarantined with measles,
face pressed to the cat-clawed screen
of my 4th floor bedroom window,
I watched the meanies next door
rip out lilacs to create a black hole
with a backhoe in their backyard.

Bigger than our elevator, the shelter came,
a shiny breadbox with a flip-top lid.
Next day at the mailboxes, the janitor cursed,
*Those cockroaches'll outlive us all
goddamn 'em to hell!*

Heedless of the rest of us rising
then raining on Cambridge, they reigned
in my night terrors: Mummy and me melting,
juggling cans of Campbell's Soup,
pleading to be let in.

Past his "Don't Block Driveway" sign,
the mister, in shiny wing tips, inspected
his lifetime guarantee, flashlight arcing like a
klieg beam over the scar that had been a garden.
Who could destroy peonies? my mother sniffed.

In thrall to the black-and-white, duck-and-cover
teachings of our new TV, I asked Jesus,
from the bed of my almost-vestigial childhood,
Where are you? as if he, who had embraced his own
mushroom cloud in ancient times, might respond.

Thought Balloon from a Funeral Home Receiving Line

Perhaps the touch of my hand might comfort?
A tender touch to say how touched I am by
your stoic smile, your touching upright posture,
and the lone untouchable tear on your eyelash?
Does my wondering make me seem a tad untouched?
Touch has never been a strength.
I felt awkward touching my mother's
arm as she died. *To touch or not to touch?*
I asked the hospice nurse. *Touch may
stall the letting go,* she said, for touch tethers
us to flesh, to warmth, to world. Who can touch
without touching beginning's end? You think,
Such fear, how sad for you! I think, *Touché.*

The Things I Cannot Change

"I accept the clangor and jangle of contrary tendencies…"
—Ralph Waldo Emerson

1.

November closes us in at both ends of the day. The sky's pallor lingers long after the sun lifts. Light's still sickly as we brush our teeth, flex stiff fingers, and step one stair at a time to the kitchen for wheat toast and a boiled egg. The newspaper on the front walk feels far away…that feeling you get when you wake looking forward to an early nap. I consider taking up smoking again. (The priest says her concept of heaven is sharing a pack of Camels with Jesus—no cough, no cancer, no guilt.) November of a year that's asked too much of us. Stolid as leathery oaks, tonight we'll toast a frosty Beaver Moon. Shelters will be full by 4:00.

2.

My church makes sandwiches for the unhoused. One slice bologna, one slice American, one packet mustard. The committee met about mayo, voted yes, but no one followed up. The addicts and addled get mustard only. One parishioner wonders how the homeless can afford cigarettes. Another snaps, *If you had no life, maybe you'd want a smoke, too!* The priest chirps, *Please, people, please.* I deliver bags of dry sandwiches at five o'clock. From the slanted shadow of the crowded porch, three huddled women chime *Thank you! Thank you! Thank you!* ("Dark though it is.") Pulling my car into my yard, I'm still considering a response.

3.

I'd made the sandwiches watching the noon news. At the Turkish consulate, a journalist met with a bone saw. Turns out, we're all collateral damage. And we're all responsible. While I slap sticky lunchmeat on white, I mute the sound of mothers wailing. Under footage of Paradise in flames, the chyron scrolls names of twelve shot dead in a college bar. On this planet, more people have cells phones than toilets, but who can you call when you're trapped in an SUV, sunroof bubbling and taillights melting? A video of a dad coaching his toddler to sing through the fire goes viral.

4.

Evening arrives before we know it; on the bones of the ash a tinge of honey lasts a moment before twilight tints clouds a palette of grays. From the forest close by, a volley of hunters' gunshots, then a hush...The coyotes are out, and so is the cat. Cardinals and chickadees lock claws around twigs to sleep standing. Sitting in the living room, snug by an apple wood fire, we raise chilled glasses to the luminary moon. Lamplight streams from neighbors' windows down the hill, and headlights strobe through tree trunks along the main road faraway. In shelters, exhausted as this aged year, guests will toss and turn...

A Glass or Two at the Five and Dime Ale House

One says, "I feel animal,
but not sexy as that sounds.
More like some mangy feral cat.
When I hear the patter of energetic
paws on the path behind me,
I whirl and snarl."

Another admits, "I'm invisible—
a widow in a Sunday pew.
They ask, 'Oh, were you in church?'
Yes! I need some assurance
there's a chance in hell I am not
a woman no man would marry."

A third, armed with one pruney
olive on a plastic mini-sword,
dismisses these confessions.
"Sooner or later, all tight buns sag.
Just ask these bar stools, girls,
and gravity doesn't care."

As if becoming unrecognizable
is a chuckle over a 4 o'clock buzz.
As if sass, jab, and bravado begin
to compensate for loss as monumental
as all that has happened since that boy
—long gone—first had me.

When I chose you, I did not know

Afternoons, we sent our narratives from the Internet café,
spinning tap-tap trips, tilapia ponds, and the antics of orphans.
Camtasia caught vodou drums beating up the valley;
we were compelled to make Americans understand.

"Nothing quenches like the precious blood of Jesus!"
the pastor declared at dinner. We blamed anti-malarials
for our furor slaked only slightly by lite-coma naps
each afternoon. We were grounded as heat lightning.

The next day we tucked a dead preemie into a dumpster
while Sister Sunshine went on rocking babies to heaven.
The nuns brought tiny green sheets for relieved
bassinets. They hung fresh feeding tubes. I hope
I will never forget what I don't want to remember.

Se ou menm ke mwen te chwazi. It is you I chose,
Haiti. You carry a basket of bruised mangoes on your head
to a village where no one buys, and even the well is thirsty.

The Yard

Around the courtyard off the cellblock, concertina wire coils. Steel pickets like pikes from some failed revolution support it, but without the befuddled, severed heads. A timeless place. It snowed this morning then rained, then the gray rain froze. When sun breaks out, icicles drip onto the concrete. When the sun goes, puddles freeze black. The incarcerated trudge through without jackets in the morgue-cold noon. Several slip and fall. Some laugh. No one helps.

> Faces lift to the haloed sun.
> A bright orange row of men—
> What will grow in this hard garden?

Lament

for the unaccompanied children

Mouths open to the moon they sleep,
lined up like new corpses on the desert floor,
backpacks as pillows in basins of pure cold.
Each searing morning, another blistering trudge,
then the train-jump. On the rusted roof of La Bestia,
they jolt past saguaro, brown river, captive towns.
This time, when the man in charge shouts run run run,
it's the boy with one unshod and bloated foot who
falls and does not get up. The children go on and on
as if the emptiness in the bowls of their bellies
is not hopelessness, as if arrival will be welcome.

Recovery

It took a façade of cake and crystallized windows,
sweet beyond anything Hansel had imagined. It took
one taste to snag him and slam him in the cage.
Turns out, he wasn't the only boy to fall
for the lie of a honey-tongued, cannibal crone.

Boys like Hansel are known for brilliant ideas—pebbles
like newly-minted dimes in the shine of a risen moon,
for half-baked schemes—breadcrumbs doomed for
the birds. And known for their reckless, headlong tasting
of the glistening. *No harm will happen to me!*

And Gretel wasn't the only girl, the only doting sister
who got by on crab-shells while her brother fattened
in his lockup on a witch's candied diet, too sated,
too amped, to fear. Sisters like Gretel fetch the water,
pail by sloshing pail, lamenting. Until they shove. Oh,

those pearls such girls may pocket? Precious inklings
of their own worth, their power to cross the river where
there is no bridge, on the back of the impossible, to carry
a brother home to a plain old house with glass windows
where once there lived a family…

You rise before the roosters to take on dangerous roads

for the refugees

When I arrived the place was filled with dust
The city of salty winds, salty tears
I, who was King of Salt at the seashore,
I planted papayas, fat belly papayas, elongated papayas
I have the godsent food of birds and an olive tree beyond the ken of
       time

We are dancing in the olive field…
While lamb was roasting and drink was flowing
Each moment is a memory renewed by a bird
Nagorno-karabakh, iraq, laos, angola, liberia, and rwanda are
The sweat of love and the sorrow that eats

I keep looking at the rice-fields, glinting in the dark
The river carries the corpse of a woman
A child wearing a small black shoe on one foot and a large blue sandal
       on the other
There are no ululations
Animals no longer speak

I think my silence means a lot
Yes. I was. Here. We all were. Yes.
I bandage my heart with the determination
       of that boy they hit with an electric stick
May you never remember & may you never forget
Be ready. Insolent guns may start again at any time

Cento Lines stitched from global poets

Hearing Loss

I wake to an inkling of finches
in the muffled maple (though sunrise trumpets
the day on our ceiling). At the front door,
hosta flutes bubble with muzzled bees.

Passing cars on the main road mimic
wind, waves, and white sound.
Lately, rain's nuance, too, is easily mistaken
for dishwasher whoosh or tinnitus static.

And what's up with consonants, particularly
plosives? They disappear in diminuendo
café conversation, leaving me marooned
with a crowd of confusing vowels.

This morning, I suspect that snap crackle and pop
I *can* hear is Time, whose annoying voice
everyone knows around town, that "Ohhh, *him!*"
from whom we all avert our eyes.

Having added more of my cochlear hair cells
to his wheelbarrow, he's trundling off to the dump
where he'll unload our non-recyclables at a bin
labeled: Common Losses.

Co-mingled, in they will slide, clattering like snowflakes.

Tenacity

A Man Who Digs Clams in Winter

When sky's arms fling wide, torching
       the horizon with wildfire,
             when sun's glacial face lifts
and nods to the edge of the continent,

the digger hauls his sled across the high tide line,
       inspecting the stitchery of rockweed fronds
            and shards of slipper shells, bronze
domes of horseshoe crab and ebony skate egg-cases.

He trudges through ice slicks and rivulets
       infused with dawn. Long johns and jacket,
            hat, hood, and gloves; his body is heavy, pure
ache. Feet and knees still bed-locked, too sore for cold's numb.

Breath steaming, he hunts for show—tiny wells where
       bivalves drink and purge. He plants his feet to dig
            the crescent of a berth, and then he rakes his run.
The rhythm warms and soothes his muscles and his mind.

The digger mines softshells brittle as porcelain.
       He curses when they chip and tosses them to the gulls
            standing by like weather vanes. In summer,
generations of clammers swap stories along the flats.

In winter, the digger's got only the clams burrowed in
       their separate black holes, each one ringed, planetary,
            solitary, all belly and muscle, hinged shut.
Two-sixteen a pound, and he's still poor. Always will be.

He looks up when he feels the tide coming up, running fast,
       moon-driven. The man glances at the day beacon,

stolid as the woman he hopes will let him in,
will keep him in safe waters. He uproots his boots.

Once

Once, I was invited to a dinner party
with Robert Lowell. Afterward, I recalled
only the grey veins in the white marble
mantle against which he leaned, tilting a gin gimlet.

"But what did he *say?*" you ask. You ask the wrong
person. You should have asked the other student poet
present that night. The lanky farmer with haystack hair
who died (when?) You know the one.

Of my childhood and the 26 thousand days since,
I remember nothing more than snippets.

Not the whole of it, the loop my years
have made. I am an eclectic character
— making a face, holding a baby,
holding hands with my one husband,

holding birthday cakes, rakes, diplomas,
picket signs, books, and a tangle of lilacs.

I hunch over snapshots in albums, asking
that woman "What is the ocean that surrounds
these islands?" Telling her: "You might not remember..."

This mist is not senescence. Even in my twenties,
I didn't remember. Here are some places I forgot:
Bloomsbury, Baja, Bordeaux...
(Though I still see a mangy German shepherd
vaulting toward my family in Hiroshima's Peace Park.)

Flashback to the children sledding our hill
in rose and navy snowsuits, or in bathing suits,

leaping off the highest quarry ledge.

My daughter waves from a rainbow parasail.
My son paddles a white-water gorge.
Nowhere, the years of carpools, office politics, home-
work, and casseroles. The day-by-day flow and

trudge. I cannot remember much of seventy
Christmases but the dead warming themselves
by a fire, the crumpling of shiny paper, the shimmery
wiggle of cranberry jelly in the shape of its can.
My lived experience slips from my mind
like a buttery egg from a Teflon pan.

That I have always forgotten continuity
suggests some incapacity,
a worrisome unworthiness
of invitations I've been sent.

My mother raised me all by herself.
I was her "Honey bee." I am her legacy.
She gripped the sharp trim
of the yellow Formica kitchen table

when she told me,
"Daddy won't be coming home again."
Decades later, when she died,
I could remember nothing else

about her than her radiant face rising,
—a smoke ring drifting through the dusty screen
of an open nursing home window.

"More than your share...

of suffering," she tells me,
intending compassion, hinting pity.
As if there is a proper portion,
as if any of us see the others
hunched over paper plates
in kitchens late on merciless nights
or slumped on deflated pillows
picking with our fingers at
slices of hard-time pie.

Tenacity

Cabin fever hauled me from our rump-sprung couch
to the oiled dirt road in a fogbank
of mosquitoes. Slapping myself blotchy, I hobbled
over forest floor debris to sit, to look,
to wake my spirit or calm it.

This is not working I told no one.
Then, in a breeze, insects vanished,
as if the air knew I needed to be there.
Just to be.

Around me,
poplars' claw-foot roots grasped boulders,
ferns unfurled from moss on stumps,
and tiny pine groves bloomed on the rocks'
humped backs: life working overtime.

So awakened and inspired,
I waited, daring some hidden hungry bear
until the mosquitoes found me ready
and drove me home as though I were
too drunk on hope to find my way alone.

Obedience

Two terracotta bowls in a gold evening, by the peonies'
full-blown white tinged-crimson—the generous blooms.
We walk the bounds of our June green yard,
cupping ashes delivered by mail—her stubborn, frugal wish—
to let our first love go. No one else is here.
Neither of us speak over *a cappella* finches
in her favorite western light.

Awful bits of bone nestle in the stonewall and dust lilts
in the lifting then settles, like dewfall drying
on the weedy, unmown grass of a lawn
as grief-struck as the lunch we attempted to cook.
We do not weep, and we do not leave—we stare out
through neighbors' yards at sails on the full blue bay.

Our tiny stash of ashes empties like the beach
at low tide, like the bottle of champagne she planned.
We stand still at the edge of where she left us.

Notes to R.

What's left of the summer you lost your grip? Only the leaves.
Letting go of the ledge, did you see light or only the leaves?

Heaped against your leaning fence, tucked in the rusting chair
where you once hoped, face upturned, there are only the leaves.

How did it come to this? you asked. For the first and only time
the last to know: our lives are not the trees, only the leaves.

Did you forget? In the school we designed out of bottles of wine
resilient children study sap and seeds, not only the leaves.

In lieu of flowers, I sent a poem. Words last longer than petals—
you wove them into crowns. Roses leave only their leaves.

My confidante you named me. But I heard your secrets
rustling in the gutters. No, that's not only the leaves.

You told my stories. Whose ears still hum with my shames?
I believed you were my cover, my shade. You only, the leaves.

Come spring, who will remind me why I will forgive you?
Who will answer your old friend's questions? Only the leaves?

Looking Up

Leaves in their beginnings:
the apple tree's chrysalides
curlicues of sugar maple
embroidery of birch.

The grass I lie in, looking up,
itches with ants on the move.
I stay put. I want to feel how
the dead would feel if they could
look up from their long work to rest
under this arc of assurances.

Excerpts from a Commencement Address to New Bullfrogs in the Pond

We've lost so many. Kudos to you few
    who sprang from your jelly cells,

      who waggling feathery gills and, fueled by
          your own tails, grew legs and lungs,
              sticky tongues and tiny fans of feet.

                 Pre-programmed to amaze,
        lazing exclamations on a sunny granite page,
you've been busy becoming!
                *

        Be ones "on whom nothing is lost."

              *

The world is full of monsters—
      the heron's pleated wingspan
         the fox's moonlit throat
            small boys with big nets
The world is full of glories—
      green glint of tickling fly
         flickering silver shiners
            wriggling gulp of worm

             *

When you move on to wider water,
      remember where you were spawned.
         Sing your silence, your baritone vibrato. Release
           your eggs, your sperm—complete yourselves.

You cannot fail.

      Your artful bodies are beneficent.

            Even when gone to snake or bird or dirt,
               you serve the common good.

Note: Thank you, Henry James, for your ubiquitous exhortation.

Martha's Faith

*"Martha, Martha, you are worried and distracted by many things;
there is need of only one thing." —Luke 10: 41-42 (NRSV)*

Holy to me are rounds of bread on the embers, my friend.
Millet cakes kneaded with mint and cinnamon,
silvery carp charring over coals in the yard.
All must be watched, turned, tended with care.
My eyes are fixed on these, my hands content
to grind the wheat, pour the wine, warm themselves
in late-day sun that sets my table with gold.

Let the Marys weep at your feet for promises
of the eternal invisible. I worship green olives
shining in a red clay bowl. Dates plumped with
honey, and cucumbers dripping earthy tears.
I can accept the notion of oblivion because
I have breathed the incense of onions sizzling
in oil I've pressed from the fruit of my soil.
Winnowing grain from the chaff, I affirm:

I believe in
the heat of the hearth,
the sweet of the fig,
the salt from the sea
in the flesh of the fish.

Nocturne

At sunset's word, night sweeps over the face
of the water like wind, loosening our moorings
to day's distractions, opening its doors
to our shadows, as boats, returning
to the harbor, disappear behind the seawall.

Now, vestigial terror drives us to light
fires to scare away beasts and memories
of beasts (eyeshine of tigers, wolf spiders, alligators,
and aged shames that make us cry aloud
triggered by a cello's broken chords.)

We generate light, for night is all around us:
dinner table tapers, votive candles in side-chapels,
gas lanterns of cobbled hill towns,
the lamp by the wing chair where I drowse
over amber brandy and sun-lit fiction.

> A full moon glints in the oak tree's crown.
> Dew silvers tall grasses.
> > Sleep tosses us

in a turbulence of dreams, twitching eyeballs
beneath eggshell lids. In the brain, synaptic
sparks meteor ideas and slide odd facts
into categories. The line of a poem missing
for months flares into view along with the dead
in their ardent faces and party dresses.

The digital clock (always at 2:22 or 3:33)
rivets insomniacs as we catastrophize:
The Call that brings a fall to pieces, a masked
anesthesiologist, the neighbor, recently kneeling

to weed dandelions, wheeled out on a stretcher...
Invasive images gaslight the hours.

Finally, finally, that silty welter settles
to the bottom of the night. Light sensitive
clouds emerge at the balancing horizon.
We rise, believing we've been spared once more
when dawn unfurls our first-born metaphor for hope.

I'm Stuck in an Elevator

But wait—it gets worse—

the passenger in the opposite corner
is my imaginary friend—

unfazed by the lurch between 10 & 11,
blonde curls highlighted with a grace note
of gray, poised and well preserved.

She's smiling like a second martini
at my frantic pounding on the buttons—
every number, even the thick red ones.

It seems an eon since I first found her
in the living room of Apartment 42,
another latch-key kid after school,

singing "If Ever I Would Leave You"
into a hairbrush mic—sharing
a passion for *Camelot*.

After that, we'd meet up at the concrete
laundry yard to thwack tennis balls
against the brick wall of #12.

She nudged me when Miss Emerson cursed
"Trouble maker!" through the cracked window—
"Thick skin, pal," she whispered. "Backbone."

Now I stop banging buttons and straighten up.

Two only-children, we'd ride bikes around
the Common into powdery hours when

our mothers worked late. People mistook us
for sisters, though I was tiny—she
my long shadow in the late low sun.

I ought to introduce myself, but I am
too embarrassed. She knows too much.
I'd like to hug, chuckle about past antics,
catch up on decades of parallel life, but—

I cannot forgive her for reminding me
what a solitary, fearful child I was. I am.

After Many Days of Rain at East Grand Lake

Cloud shadows drift like phantom fish
along the pine crown of Canada's shore,
blueing its green.

When morning light lies down
on the jutting backs of rocks, they yawn
and stretch. Lichen freckles their shoulders.

In our shallows, waves of gold rays
flicker over granite stones
where gasps of minnows shift.

The past gray days dragged tight, caught
twitching regrets on the rain's barbed hooks,
strung them and ate them for dinner.

But now sun burning through illuminates
the necessity of color; I'm relieved
it takes so little bright to brighten me.

Steel Derrick Quarry, Autumn

Working Sundays beyond the ledge top,
some townsmen and my father spent one September
putting in seedlings of hemlock and fir.
They lifted shovelsful of dirt, rooting a meadow
with young trees, packing soil back by hand.

On paths rutted by rain, I walk these afternoons.
Veteran of quarry seasons, I know fall's consolations—
collage of foliage on the woods' floor, gleaming copper,
amber, and golden sassafras. Sumac flames. Gray
cloudscapes of cliffs quivering on the surface.

In the forest hollow are traces of train tracks,
rusted as leaves. When blasting shifted granite
to building stone and aggregate, men went deaf,
machines blunt, hammering wedges. Flat cars crushed
a mile of brush hauling their weight down to the pier.

I come here for the echoes, for the familiar
mist of water meeting cooler air. It begins as breath
of resting fish, fins shifting slightly in sun refracting
off stone below. The air murmurs of underground
springs seeping slowly. I slow, imagining

the flicker of remembered men, of my spectral father,
counting trees along ledge tops. The evergreen grove
is meadow again. The granite has gone to pavers.
Schooners sailed off to museums up the coast.
At the edge, I pocket a pine cone and picture
summer's children learning to swim.

Whales in the Quarry

"When we die, let's be mama and baby whales."
—*Emily, age 5*

Imagine us
millennia from now
still swimming
in reflections of pine on sky
silk of summer nights

grays and blues
somersault and butterfly
plunge and breach

with white hands
and flipper feet
we'll slither through shallows
glide down granite stairs

breath held
I'll breaststroke deep
while you hover just above
your frail arms pale as starlight
stroking to stay in my current

You, ever my young, in this saltless sea
a glimmering moon
for her journeying mother

silver bubbles
streaming from my nostrils
trailing from your fingers

we will sing
high and low

long and slow
of hunger and danger and
staying together

forever and ever
amen

Past Tilting Signs

Driving Toward Before

These days I love—no—lust to drive.
Armed with a thermos of dark roast,
radio preset to folk tunes, I go on
all kinds of invented missions. I deliver

cookies, Cabernet, cards I might have
mailed, re-gifted jigsaw puzzles.
Dropping them by back doors,
I imagine myself a 2020 Pony Express.

I might dare to buy milk. Mostly, I just go
for a spin. Lacking a destination,
I go without navigation. All roads are open
roads past tilting CLOSED signs

on restaurants, restrooms, churches,
parking lots of parks and beaches.
Entire villages admonish me
STAY HOME! I go on, hoping

for a getaway; perhaps a place with people
strolling a boulevard past beds of tulips
planted by volunteers? Or a bar crowded with
strangers clinking bottles, cheering the team?

Windows down, I drive, adoring my wide-open
lungs full of green-gold spring. Singing praises
to sun on my hands, singing along with songs
that, back in the day, were our songs.

I drive through a country both beloved
and far from great—a gutsy, gullible, spoiled
brat of a country, growing fatter while

others scrounge in the market place

for a bouillon cube and clove of garlic.
A country immune to history's *ahas*.
A country that cannot tell the truth,
even when caught red-handed.

I drive toward the glimmer of our homeland
before it donned anger to mask despair.
Along unfamiliar empty roads, I go
nowhere as fast as I can.

Quarry Walk, 2020

What is more frightening than
a pack of teenage boys
without masks?

Back-slapping, hurling stones
like curses at the placid
water, shattering

reflections of April's tight-bud
branches and pure blue
sky. No contrails

connect the dots of continents.
Only suffering links us
Earthlings now,

and the will to live we carry—
a quiver—into what
remains of our days.

In it Together

Your great mistake is to act the drama
as if you were alone. As if death
were a sentence invented just for you.
To feel solitary is to deny
those countless others who've gone down
in the crowded ground or up in smoke—
martyrs and madmen, nurses and newborns,
Kierkegaard, James Foley and Jihadi John,
even that zealot Jesus, leaking blood and water.
Genocidaires, Gandhi, Grandpa, girls
caged in Bangkok, and, as I speak,
Fill in the blank with update people from COVID-19.
Suicides who didn't mean it. (Not to mention
the sentient others: sea stars, Monarchs, and mastodons.)
The leaves in your yard, after their last gold gasp,
layer on one another, settle, and silence
like the whoosh of the 10 p.m. train.
The regular at the bar, the neighbor
who fed your cat. Half of your book group!
The delphinium on the deck in the waning moon
was the bluest you ever saw. It's gone by.
Let go of your solitude. At the end,
in the unthinkable ineffable, everyone
is waiting for every one of us.

Election Results: We Sigh our Different Sighs

When my neighbor with his two leashed pups approaches,
we mask up and stop in the middle of our pot-holed road.

It's been awhile.

I'm worn out, he admits, shaking his head
at the state of things. *I believe the empire is falling.*

At the corner, oak leaves tap their fingers.
I'm sorry you feel that way, I say.

He is a man who charges into burning buildings
to save strangers. Who taught his daughters how to

shovel snow, construct a chicken coop, act attentive
to the forlorn old couple next door. He and I sigh our sighs.

See you. He jogs off toward town.
Be well. I shuffle toward the woods,

kicking up dust, fist-bumping an afternoon moon,
smiling out loud. Along the path, squirrels hustle

to hide samaras far from their maples. Serviceberries'
purple kernels and beads of bittersweet sow themselves

in soil and shade. I breathe in the spacious quiet of a clearing,
until drizzle clatters on the crowns of trees.

Everything is falling. Rain, night, leaves, and seeds…

After Bittersweet

I'm going after bittersweet
with a vengeance and a pair of pruners.
It's taken hold too long.

The rhizomes are beyond me,
snaking beneath the stone wall.

I lunge and tug at the wiry vines
garroting maple and grape
and moon-faced money plant.

I'm startled by how much I hate
this bittersweet.

How hard I'm yanking stems back,
snapping their necks, stabbing
their heartless hearts—

COVID and cancer, grievances
        and guns, the invasive
                damages of rage.

Mom wrenching her arm
        from Dad's brute grip,
                her fingernails shiny as berries…

Hometown

Prologue 1606

When morning mists lifted, *Talbot* passengers sighted
multitudes of mackerel, jellyfish big as sailors' faces,
and huge huffing whales. Landward: hills
of high trees and ledges shining like icebergs.
The newcomers dropped anchor,
and a tender ventured to an offshore island,
returning with berries and roses.
The people rejoiced at their safety and bounty.

* * *

Down through time, the town spun, dropping
into this Oz of a world where Whistlestop
Coffee shop is a franchise pharmacy, and the bank-
turned-bookstore a pricey residence. The poor house
is now the nursing home. Town Hall burned.
Stepping stones at low tide—the broken breakwater…
Fish shacks sell knickknacks next to the Sea Fencibles
barracks where factory art is "All sales final."

But nothing is final, really. The greater and lesser
wars swept up our Josiahs and Jimmys, as did battles
of 1812. Elms thrust muscular arms into nor'easters
along Beach Street before the blight. Now it's Ash
beetles baring the hill. Barely legible, Old Parish
Burying Ground markers name children felled
by smallpox, as COVID smothers our elders.
We are replete with grief—and light.

Such light! Light luminous on the seawall
holds us in thrall, light as compelling as first settlers'
timber, fish, and stone, beaming through

wood smoke, brine-drift, and lilacs.
We compare ourselves to granite, though
we are Atlantic swells—breaking, rising, repeating
the day-to-day coping that binds us, kind and mean
and in-between, to this here and now where we belong.

The Current Satan

For Thomas Lux

The current Satan, lacking ideology, makes it all up,
careening along like a brakeless truck toward a traffic jam.
The current Satan does not let us sleep or eat or work or love
without disorder. He slips rocks into our pockets, fentanyl
into our heroin, lethargy into our marriage. He devours hope,
the hope of the poor he taketh away with a schadenfreude grin.

The current Satan resides in the details of legal memoranda
and invests in gated communities with PRIVATE signs on
pristine beachfront. He deplores poetry but enjoys a graphic novel
Corona virus and well-placed wildfire. Receding glaciers entertain,
so, too, epic climate migrations and Murder Hornet colonies.
Scorekeeper in court, he roots for the guy in the ultimate bespoke.

Nuance isn't his forte. He's binary: *maror* not *charoset*,
mirror not window, clock-tick not birdsong.
He paid for your cartons of cigarettes.
The current Satan—and there *is* one—wants nothing to do
with the likes of you, my tender friend. You created something
called "The Perfect God." And that was when
the current Satan got pissed off.

Love, in Isolation

These days when you reach out to me
the only hand that I can hold,
we span our world entirely.
These days when you reach out to me,
remember how so desperately
we've stumbled through catastrophe.
And now, again, you steady me—
the only hand that I can hold.

The Pueblos Blancos of Andalucía

When this is over, I'll fly there, where I've never been before.
I'll find a Moorish villa with white-washed stucco walls,
bougainvillea framing every flung-wide window, an arched door
where warblers, trilling in the eaves, echo through tiled halls.

And I shall find contentment in every corner new to me.
I'll amble cobbled lanes to a plaza cantina, savor olives from Álora,
sip fresh fino sherry from a chilled glass, and glimpse a sliver of sea
glinting aqua, when I glance up from my bilingual Lorca.

I can conjugate not one verb of the language, so I won't ask *How
did the misery end? What has been lost? Who is gone?*
Trudging the rusty road to my own muted town now,
I long for warblers and bees and bell towers under an unmasked sun.

About the Author

Martha Fox published a chapbook *Tides/The Land Sighted* with poet Thomas Lux and a book *If the River's this High all Summer* (Martha Fritz, Pym-Randall Press, Cambridge, MA). She has published numerous poems in literary journals, including *The Atlantic, Comstock Review, Passager, Ploughshares, Poetry*, and *Voices and Verse*. A number of her poems are included in *Tide Lines: An Anthology of Cape Ann Poets*. After receiving a B.A. in Creative Writing from Emerson College, and an M.F.A from The University of California, Irvine, Martha was an NEA Poet in the Schools in California and continues to teach writers. Her hometown is Rockport, Massachusetts.